Breaking The Cycle:
Mental Bondage

By

Nikesha Luther

Breaking The Cycle:
Mental Bondage

Copyright by CECO Publishing

All Rights Reserved. No part of this book can be reproduced or transmitted in any form without written permission from the author.

For Booking & Contact Information:
cecopublishing@gmail.com

All scripture references are from the King James Version of the Holy Bible, unless otherwise noted.

ISBN: 978-0-9836336-1-7

Cover design by LaToya Stevens

CECO Publishing
Est. 2011

What People Are Saying About

Breaking The Cycle: Mental Bondage

"Elder Nikesha Luther embodies God's limitless capacity to help each of us to envision our journey in this life without cycles. She deposits such clear insights of awareness regarding a practical wisdom and spiritual inspiration that realigns our hearts and minds to dream again in the Lord. Our vision is made clear again."

Bishop Russell L. Freeman
United Community Cathedral Church
Columbia, Missouri

"Breaking the Cycle is a timeless work inspired by the Spirit and nurtured by Godly experience. Whether one is a layperson or of the Episcopacy, surely all walks of faith can glean from this treatise and find revitalization for pursuing their God given vision within its pages."

Elder D. Stevens
United Community Cathedral Church
Columbia, Missouri

"In this timeless book Pastor Nikesha Luther explains spiritually why vision is necessary to break the cycle of mental bondage. Moreover, she leads us into a Spirit led understanding of the dangers of misappropriating someone else's vision as our own.

In a time when believers and non-believers alike are searching for their purpose, vision, and mission in life this book encourages us to look to God to find out what He has planned for us. It provides crucial keys and practical steps to take to break the cycle of mental bondage the enemy so desires to keep us in. This work shows us that only when we pursue the purpose and walk with the vision God has for us, can we be free in our minds to live the life He has for us."

Elder LaToya Stevens
United Community Cathedral Church
Columbia, Missouri

Dedication

To my Lord and Savior Jesus Christ, the one who gives unto me the things that I cannot give to myself. I thank You for using me in ministry to reach Your people.

To my husband, Darrell, thank you for your love, support, and encouragement to do what God has called me to do. You were purposed to help bring me into position to be who I am. I am eternally grateful for you.

To Daniel and Micah, know that you can do all things through Christ who strengthens you. Your smiles are what I look forward to each morning and the inspiration to keep me going each day. I love you.

Table of Contents

Foreword
Bishop Darrell Luther   11

Prologue   13

Chapter 1
The Condition   15

Chapter 2
Establish Your Vision   22

Chapter 3
Thinking With Purpose   33

Chapter 4
Living In Harmony With Your Vision   43

Chapter 5
Operate With A Renewed Mind   56

Chapter 6
Nursing Your Vision   69

Chapter 7
Invest In Your Vision 83

Chapter 8
From Bondage To Freedom 96

Chapter 9
Keeping Your Freedom 105

FOREWORD

Co-Pastor Nikesha Luther has been released with a heaven sent word from on high concerning functions and operations that transpire in the spirit realm of the human mind. This word has been purposed and ordained to assist saints of God with the struggles and battles that are encountered in ministry and our everyday Christian walk.

It is important that in these last and evil days we embrace all insight God gives us in reference to the attacks of the enemy on our mind. For the bible says in Proverbs 23:7, "for as he thinketh within himself so is he."

Any child of God that partakes in the message found in this book will receive an enlightened word from on high that can push them into a closer connection with the Lord.

The kingdom of God has released a powerful Ministry tool found in the gifts surrounding Co-Pastor Luther. The body of Christ can certainly receive revelation knowledge that can assist in direction, place, and focus of the mind. I personally give my endorsement in the promotion of this book. Thanks goes out to Co-Pastor Luther for being a willing and yielding vessel.

Bishop Darrell D. Luther, Sr.
Senior Pastor
New Hope Christian Center
Boonville, MO, USA

PROLOGUE

The mind is a function of a person that can determine the outcome of situations that one goes through in life. If a person does not have a healthy mindset, the unhealthiness will manifest in other areas of their life. Many times, we enter into decisions, jobs, marriages, and life situations with an unhealthy mindset. A healthy mind is conducive to a positive environment, successful marriage, and a productive Christian walk. An unhealthy mind breeds disease that rapidly reproduces to touch each aspect of your walk.

If you are not healthy mentally, you will be bound and prevented from becoming healthy physically, emotionally, and spiritually. How do you know that you are unhealthy mentally? How do you begin to heal sickly areas in your life? How do you move from mental bondage to liberty? It is my intention to help you identify sick and bound areas in your life so that you can become free mentally in order to move toward your destiny in God.

Blessings
Pastor Nikesha Luther

Chapter One
The Condition

There is a power that God has given to each of us dealing with our minds. This power allows us to create, in our minds, the vision of what God has for our lives. The thought process is very important as it is a key element in determining who you are. Proverbs 23:7 tells us:

'For as he thinketh in his heart, so is he'

This power is often times misunderstood and people become disappointed because the "name it and claim it" mantra has not worked for them. It is true that what you speak can become reality for you, but *only* if it is something that God has made available to you. One must also realize that what you think in your heart is a different process than what you think in your mind. We will delve deeper into that later in this book.

Am I Mentally Bound?

When we find ourselves in mental bondage often times it is because we put ourselves in this situation. This condition can be identified with wanting to live a certain way but never seeing it become manifest in your life. You can become trapped by an idea in your imagination of what you want to be. Next thing you know, you start making decisions, you choose your mate, determine the way you run your household, and it all is chosen from your imagination. Your decisions are then made not because you are in the will of God, but because you imagined it, so then you figured it *should* be.

Let's define what I mean by imagination. Your imagination becomes active when you've tasted or seen something that you like, and then begin to desire it for yourself. Your desire can become irrational when you cannot distinguish if the thing that you desire is good or bad for you. You begin to want things that others have. You also begin to idolize people, things, and become unsatisfied with your current socioeconomic status. Unhealthy behaviors begin to appear such as gambling, stealing, gossip, abusive relationships, and addiction.

Right now is the time to identify unhealthy behaviors that you may be exhibiting. An indication of mental bondage is the inability to see your situation the same as others see it. You have to step outside of your situation and take a look at yourself from a different perspective. Is there a behavior that several people acknowledge that you exhibit, but you normally dismiss it? Are you just dealing with a situation in hopes that you can change it? Are you comfortable with where you are going and do you believe that God is pleased?

The things that are pleasing to God will yield a positive outcome in your life. Joy will abound and you will be satisfied with the things of God. Reaching for or attempting to attain things that are not in the will of God for your life, will leave you unsatisfied, angry, and resentful. Furthermore, you become extremely frustrated because that which you imagine never comes within reach. Or, when you feel that you have reached it, it turns out to be the opposite of what you hoped.

The more that you step outside of the will of God, you will begin to imagine, create, and make up a life that is not one God designed for you to live. You become restrained and constrained in a false reality that you would love to see come to pass, but will never see it!

God has designed, constructed, and fulfilled a life that has been custom made just for you. In fact, He has already spoken it! So, all that you have to do is walk in what God has designed for you. The life that God has for you is not a lifetime away. God has already given you the foundation of who you are. It is not the life that you imagine that you should have, but it is the life that you have always dreamed of!

Dreams vs. Imagination

It is very important to realize that dreams and imaginations are two separate entities. The imagination originates from the mind, but a dream originates from the heart! When two separate entities that were created to function as one, fail to function as one, it can yield dangerous results. The condition of mental bondage is rampant because the mind has not lined up with the heart.

As long as your imagination and your dreams are competing against each other, your mind and your heart can not work in conjunction with each other. Therefore, you fail to operate as you were created to operate. You become a broken Christian which allows sickness to enter the body. The body cannot fight off diseases if it is not functioning properly and there is not a unified front for a common cause.

Having your mind and heart operate in harmony with each other is possible and is crucial to you living the Christian life that you deserve to live. Extensive self-examination is required in order to identify the defects of your mind. This process will help you discern between what your will is and what the will of God is. This is the beginning of the renewal process that must take place in order to break the cycle of mental bondage.

A cycle is a series of steps taken that always ends up with the original state before the first step is taken. If your mind has not been renewed, it does not matter what direction you take or what you seemingly do differently in your situation, you will always end up in your original position.

The life that you live is filled with cycles. It is important to identify areas in your life that you feel have hindered your progress in life. Once these areas are identified, then you can begin to break the cycles that are hazardous to your destiny. The cycle of mental bondage is one that can be broken by realizing who you are, applying God's will to your life, and then living out the life that God has destined for you.

In order to do this, you must stop attempting to live what you imagine, and then begin living what you dream! How do you do this? It begins with understanding the vision that God has set forth for you. Once you uncover the vision, and begin walking in your purpose, you will find that the chains that used to keep you bound will no longer have a hold on you. The next chapter will take you on your journey to breaking the cycle of mental bondage.

Self-Awareness Check

Are you satisfied with your current situation?
_____
_____
_____

When you imagine who you would like to be, what do you see?
_____
_____
_____

What have you always dreamed that you would be? Are you that currently?
_____
_____
_____

Identify things in your life that keep you from being who God has created you to be.
_____
_____
_____

Chapter Two
Establish Your Vision

It is very easy to look at what someone else has and decide that your life should mirror theirs. They have a mansion, why can't I? They have spectacular clothes, jewelry, and cars, so why can't I have what they have? Often times we get people's lifestyles confused with the vision that God has for our own lives.

Don't Trade Your Life For Lifestyle

When God places a dream in your heart, it is the foundation of the vision for your life. Many people have dreams as children, but never set the course to ensure that the dream comes true. Instead, we look at what everyone else has, determine that the dream isn't adequate enough for us, and then abandon the dream to pursue a certain lifestyle.

It is important to look at the *life* rather than the lifestyle. Are you currently living the lifestyle that you believe that you want, but aren't happy? Are you currently not living the lifestyle that you want and remain in a miserable state? If you are not living your dream, then your lifestyle is doing nothing to progress you towards your destiny.

The style of life that you live does not determine if you are living your purpose. Just because you can buy the finer things in life, does not mean that you are living your purpose. You are not purposed to get things, you are purposed to fulfill the will of God. A new car may not be necessary to fulfill God's purpose for your life. Yes, it is nice to have it, but it will not make or break who you are in God. Many times, material things become devices that keep you from living your purpose.

Living a certain lifestyle is not detrimental to your purpose. It becomes detrimental when lifestyle begins to take the place of life. If your motivation is not dream driven, then your energy is being placed in the wrong area. Lifestyle cannot fulfill, satisfy, or complete you the way that a God-given vision can!

Let Your Dreams Re-inspire You

It is important to think back to the dreams that you once had. Why have you not sought to make them a reality? What sidetracked you in the pursuit of your dream? Did someone knock down your dream and tell you that you need to try something else?

Thinking about your dream, you must realize that God does not make mistakes! He gave you a dream, for a reason. That dream is the foundation for your vision. Just like that dream made your heart jump the first time it came to you, it makes your heart jump even now! Why? Because your spirit agrees with the dream that God has implanted in your heart.

Your dream does not have to lay dormant in your heart as a fantasy of yours. Using the creativity of your mind, you can convert what you see spiritually into something that the world can see physically. Habakkuk 2:2 tells us:

'...Write the vision, and make it plain upon tables, that he may run who readeth it.'

When you write your dream or vision down, it not only becomes real to the world, but it becomes real to you! But taking it a little further, the verse tells us to 'make it plain'. Plain means easy to recognize and without any additions. Your vision should not confuse anyone, including you. To make it plain and easy to recognize, you must construct your vision!

After you have written it, don't stop there! Take it from 2-D to 3-D. If you have to get a graphic designer to make your vision come to life for you, by all means, do it! But no longer rely on a piece of paper that you look at every morning. Instead, make your vision pop out to you. See it as you've seen it spiritually.

It is important to bring your vision to the forefront. A vision in plain sight will eliminate the peripheral vision of lifestyle! Your vision is more important than your lifestyle! Lifestyle is what sidetracks us and prevents us from living out our vision. Prosperity does not come in the form of your lifestyle, but it comes in the form of your vision! You'll become broke trying to live a certain lifestyle, but your vision will provide for you!

The vision that God implants in your heart has a purpose. It will provide for you as well as build the kingdom of God. There are Christians who are entrepreneurs, writers, influential speakers, etc., but have abandoned these skills for a 9 to 5 job because they have to pay the bills. A job sidetracks your vision from coming to fruition. Therefore, you don't live out your purpose and you begin to wonder what your purpose is.

God does not let you blindly live life without revealing to you what you were created to do. The problem lies in the failure to trust your vision, therefore failure to trust God! I'm not telling you to quit your job, but I am telling you to establish your vision! There is no better time to begin to live out your life's purpose than right now!

The Blueprint of Your Life

As you begin to establish your vision, it is important that you stay in the will of God for your life. We can always think of better things to do, or better ways to do it, but God is the ultimate architect and creator. You can't do it better than He can! The framework of your vision should be the guide to how it is fulfilled. The framework is construction from God.

With the framework in place, God gives you room to allow your creativity to flow within your vision. You can still be in the will of God and allow your creativity to give life to the vision. Once your mind is on your vision and not lifestyle, you can be able to *'prove what is that good, and acceptable, and perfect will of God'* Romans 12:2b. When inserting creativity into the framework, you must be in one of those categories for the will of God.

The good will of God is something that is approved by God. When you are filling in the framework to your vision, God will look at it and see that your creativity is good. Your vision will begin to fall into place for you, provision will come from seemingly nowhere, and God stamps His approval on you. In establishing the vision, when you are in the good will of God, you will begin to see the vision even more clearly. It will encourage you to keep moving on. If things begin to fall apart, you may want to go back to the framework. When God deems something good, it is not only good to Him, but it is good to you!

The acceptable will of God is when God is satisfied with what you are doing. You may have added something to the vision that wasn't necessarily part of the blueprint, but God accepts it and allows your vision to flourish with it. Many times we add things to our lives and the outcome does not turn out as we had hoped. This is because we have taken on something that was not acceptable to God. Therefore, he allowed it to fail so that you can purge it from your life. If something that you are doing is not working, don't try to force it to work. Again, go back to the framework to ensure that it fits with your vision.

The perfect will of God is just that, PERFECT! You may not see the perfect will of God until the vision comes into full focus for you. His perfect will is exciting because when you enter in, you will be able to discern with your spiritual eye exactly what is needed and what is not. The additions that have been made, we can determine if they should remain or if they need pruning.

The best place to be in any area of your life is in the perfect will of God. It comes later in the maturation process, but it places you in position to receive not just some, but *all* of what God has for you. When you are in the perfect will of God, a job can't hold you back, people can't hold you back, but you rely completely on the sustaining power of God!

Fulfilling Your Vision Takes Time

While you are on your journey to living your vision, do not get weary! Habakkuk 2:3 tells us:

'For the vision is yet for an appointed time, but at the end it shall speak, and not lie; though it tarry, wait for it; because it will surely come, it will not tarry.'

When your vision is fulfilled, it will not only help build the kingdom of God, but it will accomplish the purpose that God has for your life. This is a big deal! Your vision is not one that you can visit for one day and expect everything to fall into place. But, you have to work what God has given you. This will not happen overnight!

Identifying defects in the way that you think and then realizing your vision are just the first steps that one has to take in the process of breaking free of bondage. Bondage is not a permanent state and vision will bring you liberty.

Establishing your vision is a key component of breaking the cycle of mental bondage. It gives you a focus area to begin moving into the destiny that God has for you. Establishing the vision is good, but there is still work to do!

Self –Awareness Check

What has always been your dream?

_____

_____

_____

What kind of life do you want to live?

_____

_____

_____

Identify the things that have sidetracked you from your dream.

_____

_____

_____

Plainly state your vision.

_____

_____

_____

Chapter Three
Thinking with Purpose

God has given you a vision and you write it on the wall for everyone to see. You know this vision because it was birthed within your heart. You have an intimate relationship with it and you are just the person to grow it to become your destiny. But, like many visions, yours is still on the wall, doing nothing. Also, like other visions, it has become partially covered, if not completely covered, by other things in your life. It is not enough to establish your vision; you must also BELIEVE your vision!

Believe in Your Heart

Believing in your vision is the next step to bring you out of mental bondage. If you don't believe in something, you won't do what it takes to support and help it to grow. God gave you the vision, so there is no doubt that He will make a way for it to be manifested. Yet, doubt is readily lurking!

The belief that you possess is contingent upon your faith that God will do what He said that He will. We often times are disappointed because we put our faith in people, and of course, they have failed us. However, faith in God is an investment that promises to yield a return. In order to yield a return, you must first invest!

How do you invest in God? You take the most valuable thing to you and give it over to God. The very thing that God gave you, you must give it back to Him. When you accepted Christ, and He freed you from the bondage of sin, He gave you your life back! Your life was once in the grasp of sin and you could not be released on your own. Jesus snatched you from a death grip and allowed you to live in liberty. In return for Him saving you, give yourself back to Him!

Believing is not something that you can think, "I'm going to believe God today!" That sounds good, but you and I both know that it doesn't happen that way. The moment you say that, thoughts come into your head and try to persuade you otherwise. Believing takes dedication. In fact, in order for you to believe, you have to *know* that what you believe is true!

When God gives you a vision, He implants it in such a way that you know that it is from God! He does this so that you believe that you are the vessel to bring the vision to light! When you think on your vision, you have to know that the vision is from God. You have to know that He gave it just for you. If you don't know that it is true, you will not believe in your vision, and you won't do anything to support it!

Think Positively

You can't believe in something that you don't have positive thoughts on. If you can't think of positive things that come from your vision, it will not become important to you and your vision will die. We can suffocate our visions by covering them with thoughts that do nothing to help them come to pass. Because your dream originates in the heart, your heart is needed in order for you to see the vision physically.

It is important not to think and build with your mind alone. If your heart is not involved in the thought process, then the vision will lose the very core of itself. You will be left with a meaningless creation that fails to do what you had imagined it to do. Your thoughts are crucial to bringing your vision to life. It is important to distinguish the way your mind thinks and the way that your heart thinks!

The mind is a vehicle that fuels the creative juices. It can think of several ways to do one function. It is very complex and very simple at the same time. The mind can become independent of the body. This is why you can work a job that requires your full attention and still enter into a different world by daydreaming. Because the mind can become independent, it is the perfect battleground!

An independent mind, that is not focused on what the body is doing, can run rampant within itself. The devil manipulates the mind just by whispering suggestions into it. The devil has won many battles by catching people in an independent state. We see the mind as a potential battlefield, but the devil sees it as a playground. As long as your mind is not focused on your vision, it is simple enough to be attacked just by simple suggestion.

Through the gateway of the mind, the devil can bind as many people as he chooses. He can suggest that you are better than where you are and then give you an idea that will take you completely away from the life that you are destined to live. He can tell you that you can change the person that is verbally and physically abusing you, so you stay in that relationship. He can speak to you so often that you don't hear what God is trying to tell you.

It is very dangerous to think outside of the vision that God has given you. If you allow your mind to stay independent, it will fall into a pseudo-freedom. It will make you think that you are living your life and 'doing you', but instead you are living in a fantasy world that you can't break from. But after you establish your vision, and you become focused on what God has for you, you can shift from thinking with your mind to thinking with your heart.

Impurities Free Thinking

Thinking with your heart is NOT an emotion. Emotions originate from the mind. When women are in abusive relationships they often say, 'My mind is telling me to leave him, but my heart is telling me that I love him too much'. People mistakenly equate the heart with emotion, which can keep them bound mentally! What these women don't realize is that their heart is telling them to leave, while the mind is telling them to stay. When you think with your heart, you think with truth. When your heart and your mind are not lining up with each other, it is a true indication that there is battle going on.

The heart is the very core of you. When you accept Jesus Christ as your Savior, the heart is also the place where He dwells. You cannot go wrong when your thoughts are purposed toward your vision because the vision originates in the heart. When your thinking is coming from your heart, then it is free from impurities.

Until your thoughts are associated with your purpose, you will not accomplish your vision. When your thoughts are centered on your purpose, the things that would normally bind you will be of no effect! Debt, bondage, and control can all be broken by your thoughts. How? Your thoughts determine your circumstances. When you think on your vision, your thoughts are healthy.

Your vision is something that is pure because it is given by God. So when your thoughts are pure, you won't desire anything that is impure. When you believe in your vision, you don't want anything to come in to warp or destroy it.

As you work on your vision, because of the purity of your actions, your nature will be affected! Your thoughts will be healthy which will establish health mentally, physically and spiritually. As you keep your vision before you, you keep the promise in the forefront. Your vision gives you joy. As long as you dwell on joy, you will have joy!

Bring Discipline to Your Thoughts

Purposed thinking requires discipline and prayer. Because there is a constant attack on your mind, you have to purposely direct your heart to think! The devil cannot get to your heart because he cannot overtake a place where Jesus dwells; although that is what he wants. He wants the core of you. So if he can get you to move your thoughts from your heart to your mind, he can gain some control.

But he can be defeated once you align the thoughts of your mind with your heart. Once you feel yourself thinking with your mind, you should check yourself and begin to do some heart thinking! Think on the love that God has for you. Think on the vision for your life. When you begin to discipline your thoughts, you will begin to break free from any bondage that may have you tied up mentally.

Disciplined thoughts will also encourage an intimate relationship with God. As you pay attention to your thinking, you can direct yourself to pray more, to meditate more, and to enter into God's presence. With your heart leading your thoughts, Jesus will become the center of your life.

With Jesus as the center, the impossible will become possible for you. As you purpose your thinking towards your vision, God will begin to make provision for you. Those things that you think, you will begin to have. Why? Because your thinking is not centered on lifestyle, but your thinking is centered on your vision. Your vision is God given and therefore you will be thinking and operating in the perfect will of God. His will is that you have a personal relationship with Him, that you do not allow self to get in the way of your destiny, and that you accept Jesus as your Savior.

When you think with purpose, you will think with clarity. Your decision-making will become purposed, your walk will become purposed, and your life will become purposed. You will truly walk in your purpose. Walking in your purpose will allow you to continue to build on the vision that God has purposed for you.

Knowing your vision is one thing, but living your vision is another. You have made a life outside of your vision. How do you connect your present life to the vision that God has before you?

Self-Awareness Check

Looking at your vision, do you believe in it? Why or why not?

_____

_____

How will your vision impact the kingdom of God?

_____

_____

How can you begin to focus on positivity?

_____

_____

Create a mini schedule that will help you become disciplined in prayer.

_____

_____

_____

Chapter Four
Living In Harmony with Your Vision

As you begin to align your life with your vision, you will see things that you have allowed to enter into your life that are outside of the will of God. During the process of breaking through the state of mental bondage, your vision will become more evident. This means that purging must take place, even if it seems overwhelming at first.

Living In Spite of Your Vision

We have all done it. We know there is something pressing us to move, to do what we know is in our hearts. But, there is a little something called life that seemingly prevents us from doing what we are called to do. Instead of doing what we feel we should do, we end up doing what we feel we *have* to do.

What are the things that we have to do? We have to go to work, school, clean, take care of the kids, etc. The list will go on and on. We have become a people of doing everything except what we are called to do. Why is this?

We have taken things that are a part of our lives and made them our lives. Although you love your kids, they aren't your life. Your spouse is your partner, but he/she is not your life. In fact, your life isn't even yours! What are you doing with the life that is not yours to begin with? Are you making the most out of life or are you just making a life?

When we live without vision, we live without the guidance of the Holy Spirit. You cannot lead and guide yourself to the truth. That is the job of the Holy Spirit. No matter how skilled you are, you are not proficient in this area. However, when you choose to live by your standards alone, you are attempting to lead and guide yourself. Proverbs 29:18a tells us:

'Where there is no vision, the people perish'

Where there is no vision, you will utterly fail. Without a foundation, what falls cannot be resurrected. You can have the greatest idea in the world, but if God didn't release the vision to you, you will just have a great idea.

Many times we take that great idea and go a route completely different than what God has intended us to go. This idea, then, takes us back to the cycle of mental bondage. We begin to imagine ourselves somewhere or doing something that God has not intended for us.

When you neglect the vision that God has given you and opt to live a life that you construct for yourself, it is like lacing your plans with C-4. At any moment the remote can detonate and your plans will blow up in your face.

You must realize that things that blow up in your face do not mean death to your vision. Instead, it makes way for your vision! When cycles are broken, you actually feel the impact. You feel the blow because if you didn't, you would try to rebuild the very thing that God destroyed for your good. Yes, sometimes God has to blow some things up in our lives to bring us back to Him. When you live in spite of your vision, you live in spite of God. What does spite mean? It means malice or hatred. You live like you hate what God has laid out for you, so you resort to finding something that you feel best suits you.

I know that seems pretty extreme but when you rely on anything other than God, He sees that as a rejection. You know there is something tugging at your heart to do, but you ignore it to do something else. God is pointing you down a certain path, but you can't see two steps in front of you, so you go the other way. If you fall into this category, it is not too late to begin living your vision!

Living Because of Your Vision

Many times, when we think of our vision, we become intimidated by the thought of actually doing something that is purposed for the life that we live. Who wouldn't want to live out their dreams? That is a question that we ask ourselves many times over the span of our lives. Normally, it is a question that is spoken into the atmosphere, but there is no action associated with it.

It's true that it takes hard work to realize and live out your vision. The hard work should not be a deterrent to achieving your vision. In fact, it should be an encouragement to actually begin to do what is necessary to make sure that your vision becomes a reality.

The best way to live in line with your vision is to begin the moment that it is implanted in your heart. Well, most of us received the vision early in life, so it is harder to live towards the vision. Why? If you have not kept your vision in the forefront, then it is now resting under a 1000 ton pile of life.

In order to get to your vision, you have to begin to throw away all of the excess buildup that is preventing you from living your vision. Through determination, commitment, support, and love, you will be able to live your life according to your vision.

What does this mean? Those relationships that mean you no good, the things that keep you in debt, things that take your smile away from you, these are the things that you have to peel away so that you have a pure focus on your purpose.

Yes, this will be very hard and at times painful. But when you know that there is good beneath the pain, it is an incentive to begin purging your life of all things that are unnecessary. Know that as you pluck out all of the unsightly things, it makes what is left even the more beautiful. It makes it even the more appealing. It will give you the desire to make your vision come to pass.

As your vision becomes appealing to you, your life should be lived according to the structure of the vision. If it is not required for your vision to come to pass, why buy it? If they don't believe in your vision, why keep them in your circle? These are questions that you should ask yourself as you live according to the vision.

The decision making process should become easier for you. Many times, we make decisions for the short term. But with a vision structure in place, your decision can be for the long term. You'll begin to know what is needed as it comes along. God will provide for you in every area of your life. There are times when we miss the provision because our focus is not on the vision that He gave us. It may not seem as though you need it right now, but maybe it was presented to you for a reason. Think back on the times when something was made available to you, you passed it up, and later you wished that you had taken it.

The focus that you apply to your vision will allow you to discern what you need and what you want. Need comes from your heart knowing what is necessary to fulfill your purpose. Want comes from your mind trying to live a certain lifestyle. It is important to put your needs before your wants. As long as your needs are taken care of, your wants will not have the position to control your life.

You can become addicted to wants if you don't practice self-control! People who give wants the number one position in their life, end up becoming one or more of the '-holics'; shopaholics, alcoholics, etc. Wants can take over your life if you don't ensure that your needs are taken care of.

Once you begin living solely to fulfill your purpose, to see your vision realized, to fulfill God's will for your life, your living will not be in vain. God will provide for you so incredibly, that your provision will have provisions! Focusing your eyes in the same direction as God's eyes will make the impossible possible for you!

Aligning Yourself With God's Will

It can be difficult at times to understand what exactly God wants you to do. Ok, so you have the vision, it looks good, but how do you know what God wants you to do next?

Following your life according to the will of God is not a complicated procedure. We often take our comforter, the Holy Spirit, for granted. He is there for us at any time, but we fail to call upon the supernatural guidance that He can provide.

It is as simple as asking God to help you, to show you the way. The thing about God is if you ask for Him to show up, He will definitely show up. But you have to be able to trust that everything that He positions in front of you is to help you and not to harm you.

You can't align yourself with the will of God if you don't have a relationship with Him. He desires that you love Him with all of you! That means that every area of your life has God at the center. If you find it difficult to believe God is pleased with something that you are doing, then you have to realize that He is not the center and you are in need of realignment.

Without prayer and meditation, there is no drive for the vision. It is one thing to know what God would have you to do, but if you don't practice what is needed to sustain you on your journey, you will give out as soon as you start. God's will is that you build yourself up spiritually in order to go the distance with your vision.

There are things that you have to obtain from the spirit realm in order to operate in the physical. What do I mean by this? You are not just made up of a physical man alone. If you don't pour into your spirit man, you become an unbalanced person. In order to balance yourself out, you have to go to God to feed you spiritually. You have to build up your most holy faith in order to ensure that the vision comes to pass.

Once your spirit and your physical man are in position to operate together, then and only then will you operate at the best capacity that you were made for. This is the alignment that is needed in order to be in the will of God. It is important that your physical health is not the end to your exercise regimen. If the spirit is not included, then you may as well not exercise at all.

God's will is simple. The righteousness that He has presented in you will recognize the will of God. It takes getting your flesh into subjection in order to keep God's will first and yours second. The character of God should show up in your character. He desires that we carry ourselves, think, and act the way that He would.

The popular phrase in the 1990's 'What Would Jesus Do?' is one that is worth revisiting. If God wouldn't be pleased with you doing something, it is best that you don't do it. Simple to say, I know, but it is the only way to keep your mind on your vision. Questioning whether God will approve of your decisions or actions will intentionally move your thought process to the things of God. Therefore, the will of God is in the forefront and you will most likely begin to live and look like Him!

Respect For Your Vision

It is important to realize that what God has given you in the form of a vision is something so precious and key to your destiny that you have to treat it as such. It is something that is worth protecting.

Protect your vision as you would protect a child. Your vision is something that grows, needs nurturing, attention, and has the potential to make an extraordinary impact in you as well as the lives of others. It is so important that your vision comes to reality, that even if you abandon it, it still remains in your heart.

The vision that God gives you is a living testament to the power of God. You should not look upon it as something menial and not worthy of your utmost respect. In fact, you should not allow anyone to downplay what God has set forth for your life.

The things of God are awesome, and it is such a privilege to be the bearer of something that was given straight from God. Your vision should not be tossed to the wayside or put on the back burner of your life. It was given because there is a need for it to be fulfilled and you are just the vessel to fulfill it.

Take pride in what God has given you. It may not look like what someone else has, but it is yours. It may not seem as though it would mean much, however, if you look at it through spiritual eyes, I know that you will see the impact that your vision will bring. Your vision is designed to build the kingdom of God. If you don't respect it and take it seriously, then who will?

Self-Awareness Check

How has your life deviated from your vision?

_____

_____

_____

Identify 4 things that are excess buildup in your life.

_____

_____

_____

How can you rid yourself of the buildup?

_____

_____

_____

How will you balance yourself physically and spiritually?

_____

_____

_____

Chapter Five
Operating With A Renewed Mind

Change is something that many people struggle with. The motto 'If it isn't broken, don't fix it' comes to mind when change invokes negative responses within people. If you want to live out the purpose for your life, there are some things that will have to change currently. Also, you have to realize that change doesn't happen overnight, even when you are determined to do what God has told you to do.

Newness Is A Process

It would be extremely difficult for you if someone commanded you to stop what you are doing now and change things to meet their requirements. There are habits that we are used to, we sleep on a certain side of the bed, and we eat a cookie a specific way each time. We are creatures of habit.

Because we have habits, it is important to take a look at them one at a time. If you try to change everything about your life in one day, you will be a nervous wreck. There is a certain order to your life, whether it is healthy or unhealthy for you. Just like babies have to be weaned off of milk, you have to be weaned off of your bad habits. Why? This is because if you move too quickly, you may not have severed the link between you and your habit. This is why people can temporarily quit smoking, but something happens and they pick up a cigarette out of *habit*!

A process is a series of steps that someone must take in order to achieve a desired result. The saying goes that 'old habits die hard'. This may seem negative to the people that use this saying, however I have found hope in it. The hope is that it may be a hard death, but old habits can die. This means that there is opportunity for newness to be created in your life. This also means that the old does not have to live with you anymore!

The first step to newness is aligning your thought process up with new. If you think and act old, you will walk and talk old, and then the only way anyone can describe you would be to call you old! You have got to think, embrace, and love all things new! As you think on new, an amazing thing will happen. You will no longer give as much time to the old. I didn't say that you will no longer think about the old, but you will spend less time thinking about it.

The biggest thing that keeps people from moving forward into their destiny is worry, pain, and negative thoughts from the past. You will never forget your past; things may have hurt you, or things even may have been great in the past. But one thing is for sure, you cannot get your past back. Even if you try to recreate the circumstances of your past, it will not be the same, because you are not the same. You would not be able to operate like you did if your present self was inserted into your past. You've grown more, experienced more, learned more, and you have more to give and offer yourself.

While you line up your thought process with new, you have to abandon the old world of your past. Your past can hijack your future if you can't let go of what was and focus on what is to come. Your past has passed; your vision is your future!

Secondly, you have got to examine your life. What is operating presently in your life that is linked to the old you? This can be friends, emotions, places that you visit, or even family members. Things that you used to do, people that you used to talk to, and places that you used to go may not be able to make it into the newness that God has for you.

When you make it up in your mind to dump some things that are hindering you, you may end up with a lot of space. This space used to be inhabited by things that did nothing to help drive you towards your purpose. When the space appears, don't immediately replace it with something else. Give yourself time to adjust to the extra time that God has given you. You will need it as you begin to unravel your vision.

Lastly, understand that God knows that you are a work in progress. However, you should continue to progress and not use your current status as a crutch to go back to the old. Falling may result in bruises, but it won't make your vision leave you. You can abandon your vision, but your vision won't abandon you. If you are determined to do what you are called to do, that determination will lead you into your destiny. Your vision is strong enough to catch you. That is why God created the vision just for you. It can handle your slips and falls every now and then, and it is ready for you when you come out of the old.

God has given you a vision that can't get old. It is living. As you progress, it progresses with you. The everlasting newness of your vision will give you vast opportunities to get your mind off of the old and focused on the new.

Old Contaminates New

People often reminisce about the 'good old days' where a person didn't have a care in the world. You could go outside and feel safe. You could ride in your car without a seatbelt. Life was good back then. However, no one really talks about the deadly car crashes, the kidnappings, or the struggles when they talk about the good old days.

The things that go on today are the same things that went on back then. Now, as things have changed and technology has gotten better, it is easier to do the things that were done back then. The things of the old days never died, they regrouped and got stronger as we entered into new days.

This is a reminder that even though your tomorrow is brighter, yesterday's rain could affect it if you allow it to. Matthew 9:17 tells us:

'Neither do men put new wine into old bottles: else the bottles break, and the wine runneth out, and the bottles perish: but they put new wine in new bottles, and both are preserved.'

Old things have the ability to rot things that are new! If you enter into a new relationship, compare the new to the old, and then act as though the new relationship will be just like the old, then the new will be destroyed. What am I saying? You cannot operate with a renewed mind and continue doing the things that you used to do.

In college, I used to go to clubs or parties every weekend. That is something that I could do while I was in my old bottle. If someone told me that I shouldn't do those things, it would be poured into my bottle, but it would quickly run out. New things may not be accepted if everything else is old! I had to completely let go of what I was doing in order to move forward in newness. Am I able to go to clubs now? Yes! However, I won't because my purpose will not allow me to! I have a new bottle and I can't allow the old to destroy the new work that God has established in me!

This is why when an organization decides to make a change for the better, they don't just make the change and keep everything else the same. They will take the organization through a complete restructuring. If they don't, then the old will contaminate the new so much, that you wouldn't be able to tell that anything had changed.

When you decide to make a change, everything that is linked to that change should also go through a renewing process. Don't allow that old dust to get onto your newness. Keep your newness clean by keeping old things away from it!

The Pruning Process

When you begin to operate in newness, your focus will be so clear that the things that hinder you will begin to stand out like a sore thumb. You will begin to actually hear how people talk around you. Conversations that used to be degrading and funny will make you think twice. This is because God is taking you to a level where you will begin to understand that your purpose will affect the lives of people.

Accountability and responsibility for what you are attached to will become a priority in your life. This means that you have to be careful of who is around you and what stake they have in hindering or progressing your vision.

Some things that may be issues in your life are easy to find and cut out. However, there may be some things that have grown with you that you never thought would hinder your progress in God. Those are the things that can be the most dangerous to your vision; the hindrances that are hiding in plain sight.

It is important to allow God to lead you in pruning things from your life. Many times, we can get scissor happy and begin to cut things that are valuable to the vision. Just because that person gets on your last nerve does not mean that he or she should be cut out of your life. Your opinion no longer matters; it is the will of God that has to be supreme in your decision making.

In order to ensure that you are pruning the right things, you have to look at what is being produced. Are holy things being produced or are evil things being produced? It is not hard to distinguish if the fruit is of God or not. We just have to be willing to let go of the things that mean us no good.

If I have a friend that is always upset and wants me to be upset with them, then that friend is someone that I may have to prune. When you take on someone else's offense or anger, you are no longer looking at your vision, but are distracted by something that is not of God.

When I speak of pruning, I don't mean to just throw someone away. However, I do mean that you should take away the influence that they have over your life. It is ok to continue to pray for someone, but if you are not strong enough to hear about everything that is going wrong in their lives without being affected, then the conversation must be pruned.

As you begin the pruning process, little by little, the things that once clouded your vision will be moved out of your line of sight. It will not only allow you to see more clearly, but you will be able to operate easier. It will be easier because the load of dead things in your life will be removed, making way for newness to be poured into you!

Space to Grow

It is something about removing things from an area and sitting back and seeing all of the space that you thought that you didn't have. Cleaning a room brightens it and makes it more inviting. The very act of cleaning even changes the atmosphere of the room.

When you operate in a renewed mind, you are operating in a way that you have never operated before. You smile more and you don't miss the things that used to hold you down. It is important that you allow God to work with the newly found space in your life. It is very easy to clutter up a room that has been cleaned. The same thing can happen with your mind. If you don't keep it renewed, it can easily be filled with things that can cause clutter.

After the pruning process, space is available in your life. This space is reserved for the things needed in order to accomplish your vision. It is important to protect the newly found space. You have to be careful who you allow in. It is not meant for you to turn everyone away, but you have to be selective in who has access to the things of the vision.

You may have had time allotted to spend time with a friend that you had to remove due to the pruning process. That time should not be filled being idle, but it should be used for growth. We have to be mindful that the mind is a battlefield for the devil. If you don't protect it when it is renewed, he can suggest that you do something that is outside of the will of God and then you will find yourself doing it.

When God allows space and growth in your life, it is a time to take advantage of it. Our lives are filled with complexities, things that make us rush through the day, and we sometimes feel as though nothing was accomplished. When you allow God to renew your mind, things in your life will become new. The old has GOT to pass away and new things, new opportunities, and a new mind will be available to you. Space does not mean it is ok to stop being productive, but space is an indication that something will be planted to further your growth.

Operating in a renewed mind will affect all aspects of your life. It will cause you to identify and remove things that are a hindrance to your destiny. It will also give you a clearer focus on your vision. Thank God for renewing your mind! Going through life with a heavy load to bear is something that is not meant for you. Being bound mentally is a heavy load. Allow God to break you free of that! Once you are operating in a renewed mind and have broken free mentally, breathing comes so much easier!

Self-Awareness Check

What are some habits that you need to break?

_____

_____

How has your past affected your future?

_____

_____

What are you dealing with that is linked to your past?

_____

_____

What changes do you need to make?

_____

_____

_____

Chapter Six
Nursing Your Vision

It is such a relief to become mentally free. But, once you are free, what do you do with the vision for your life? How can you make sure that you don't fall back into bondage? Your vision, your purpose, is like your baby. If you don't nurse it, it will not live. There are things that you have to do in order for your vision to stay alive and breathing. As an illustration, I will utilize the story in 1 Kings Chapter 3.

Protect Your Vision

When God reveals what your purpose is, your actions will determine how that purpose manifests in your life. How you handle your purpose will determine how you reach your destiny.

You have to be purposely aware that your vision is with you at all times. Earlier, we talked about the vision being at the bottom of the pile of everything else in your life. It is very easy to forget that you have a purpose for your life if it is not kept before you.

You can actually smother your vision by not being aware of it. We can liken this to a mother nursing her child in bed. There is a thing called mother's intuition where a mother is aware of her child at all times and therefore is able to nurse, while she is sleeping, with the baby beside her. However, there have been reports of mothers killing their child by rolling over on top of them.

There is something very important to learn from this. Your vision should be so much a part of you, that you are aware of it even when you are asleep! However, some of us are sleeping so deeply on our vision that we are killing our purpose. 1 Kings 3:19 tells us:

'And this woman's child died in the night; because she overlaid it.'

It is a good thing to get rest. But, when you oversleep, it can be detrimental to your purpose. When you oversleep, your responsibilities are neglected, things are left undone, and time seems to slip away from you. Before you know it, you have forgotten about your vision, and therefore, your purpose is not being fulfilled. This begins the cycle of mental bondage all over again. Because the vision has suffocated, now there is no focus, and the devil can begin to suggest things to you and before you know it, you are bound again!

However, while you are resting, you can still protect the vision that God has given you. Protecting your vision means that anything that could have the potential of harming it has got to go! You have to be aware of surroundings. You wouldn't allow your child to just go anywhere that they wanted to. There are boundaries that we set for children for a reason. Because the vision lies within you, there should be boundaries that you set for yourself.

If you look at verse 19, it is important to see when the child died. He died at *night*! The time of day that your vision is most vulnerable is at night. Why is that? It is because your vision isn't as visible at night. When it is daytime, people can see where you are and they can know what you are doing. But the night hours can bring about secrecy and allow people do things that they would not do during the day.

This may seem a little drastic, however it is important to realize that if you are just being released from mental bondage, your time should not be spent in the streets at all hours of the night. Just like a child has a curfew, you may want to set one for yourself.

The enemy wreaks havoc at midnight. The devil knows that you are less aware of your purpose at night, so he cannot wait to meet you with your guard down. If protecting your purpose means that the nightlife is not for you, then make sure that your curfew is intact.

Christians become stronger and stronger everyday as they protect and nurture their vision. The only way that you can stand the wiles of the devil is if your focus is on your purpose, therefore your focus is on God.

Protect your vision with all of your might! It is your child that must grow and then make way for you. As you are protecting your vision, you have to make sure that you intimately know what you are protecting. The devil is out to steal, kill, and destroy, and if you are not familiar with your vision, it can become a prime target for the enemy.

The Alternate Vision

Protecting your vision means that you are careful of your visions at all times. Nursing mothers have the ability to know where their child is, but sometimes the mind can wander. Still, you can allow your vision to be vulnerable due to carelessness. 1 Kings 3:20 tells us:

'And she arose at midnight, and took my son from beside me, while thine handmaid slept, and laid it in her bosom, and laid her dead child in my bosom.'

Did you see that? Because she slept carelessly, someone was able to come into her bed, take her child, and then replace it with one that was dead! You can be in the position where the devil can have access to your purpose and then hijack it! But the devil is so cunning that he won't just leave you with anything. He we will send you a replacement vision!

This happens when we choose to live life outside of the vision that God has for us. Even if the life that you are living seems like it is Godly, as long as you are not living the purpose that God has for you, the devil is happy! Why? Because your vision was designed just for you and there is power that comes along with it. If he can hijack your vision, your power, and replace it with something that is not yours, he has accomplished his purpose for your life.

This is the reason why when you try to accomplish things outside of your vision, it seemingly fails every time. You have power to bring your vision to fruition, but that power is designated to your vision. You cannot use that power on something that is not yours!

The devil is ok with you working a vision that is not yours, because the potential power that you have won't work with what he gives you. If he can distract you from your purpose with a purpose that is not yours, he can prevent you from entering into your destiny.

Once again, you will be in the position to become mentally bound. It is very difficult for a person to have a vision in their head, but no matter what they do, the vision never comes to pass. It can make you give up on life, abandon the pursuit of your purpose, and ultimately give up on God.

If you find yourself struggling in the pursuit of your vision, you may want to go back to the drawing board. There is a level of difficulty when trying to live your purpose, but it is not impossible. God created you and He created a vision just for you. It fits you perfectly and you are just the person to make it a reality. He would not give you something that you could not make work.

The devil's purpose is to steal, kill, and destroy. However, you have the vision and the purpose to ensure he is not successful. As you become intimate with your vision, you should be able to recognize if the vision you are working is yours or if it is counterfeit from the devil.

Who's Vision Are You Nursing

Many times, instead of pursuing our own vision, we sit and nurse someone else's dead child.

It is important to note that I am not referring to the vision of the church that you go to. That vision is something that the fellowship must ensure comes to pass. I'm only speaking of your personal vision and ensuring that you are doing what God has put in your heart and not a substitute.

When we begin to nurse a counterfeit vision, it usually entails settling for something that is not yours. God has given you a living vision, so that means that you deserve better than something that is dead. When you are nursing a vision, you should be able to discern if the vision is truly yours or not.

God will let you know if your vision has been tampered with. If what you are doing has the opposite result of what was intended, then you may want to consider if it is *your* vision. If you continually try to put your all into your vision, and it is not moving, you may want to check the pulse. If the vision has no pulse, then you have to check if it is truly your vision. 1 Kings 3:21 tells us:

'And when I rose in the morning to give my child suck, behold, it was dead: but when I had considered it in the morning, behold, it was not my son, which I did bear.'

If the vision that you are working is not bearing any fruit, it is important to not give up. If you recognize that the vision that you are nursing is dead, also recognize what your purpose is. If the vision and purpose are in conflict with each other, you have got to look a little closer. When the night hours faded away, she was able to see the child for what it truly was.

The woman was careless during the night and as a result of her carelessness, her baby was exchanged for a dead child. But look, she did not resign herself to that fact. She felt that something was not right, so she looked a little closer and discovered that it was indeed not her child.

Like the woman, you must look closely at your vision. Then, take a second to look at what you are doing. Is what I am attempting to accomplish really mine to accomplish? I know that God has promised me vision, but why do I see failure in everything that I touch? Plainly put, you cannot successfully operate in a purpose that is not yours.

When you operate in a dead purpose, you will receive dead things from it. Something dead cannot produce life; in fact it can bind you up with bitterness, failure, and anger. When God sends you a vision, that vision cannot produce death, it can only produce life.

When you recognize that you are nursing something that is not yours, you have to immediately stop feeding it and find what is yours! You have to stop giving your time and energy to things that only bring you misery. Some people are so wrapped up in something that is not theirs, which they often settle for it because it is the only thing that they know.

Pumping your time into something that is dead will not cause it to live. It may cause it to move and operate as if it is alive, but it will actually be something that is dead walking. A substitution for the real thing is not the real thing. A bad relationship that leads to marriage will not produce the fruit that a Godly marriage produces. It may look good on the outside, but the inside can be in a sickly, rotten condition. There are things that you have to leave in order to give the attention needed for your vision.

Ensure That the Vision Lives

When you come into the realization that you are operating your vision, you must ensure that the vision lives at all costs. You will protect something that is dear to your heart. Even if you have to let it go for a while, you will make sure that it is taken care of. That is the level of intimacy that you should have with your vision. No matter what happens to you, you should make sure that the vision lives.

The vision that God gives you may not be just for the short time that you live on earth. But, it will produce fruit for ages to come. There is importance and potential that is placed on your life, therefore your vision carries the same characteristics with it. Your vision must remain intact. 1 Kings 3:27 tells us:

'Then the king answered and said, Give her the living child, and in no wise slay it: she is the mother thereof.'

After you recognize that the enemy has already replaced or is attempting to replace your vision with something else, know that he will not willingly give it back to you. These two women both laid claim on the child that was alive. They both defended themselves to the king in order to keep the child.

However, the woman that stole the child really did not care for him and did not care what happened to him. It is important that you do not allow someone who does not care for your vision to come in and contaminate what you are doing. Just because you have a vision does not mean that everyone will accept it.

What is funny is that these two women lived together. They had a relationship with each other. In fact, they couldn't depend on anyone else but each other. The very person that you think is for you could be against you. This takes us back to the beginning of this chapter; you have to protect what God gives you!

Don't allow anyone to destroy what God has given you. Even if it comes to someone trying to take it, don't allow them to destroy it. As long as it lives, you will have fulfilled your purpose. Take comfort in knowing that no one can work your vision that way that you can.

The child was the woman's only child. She wanted that child to have life even if she was not the one providing for him. God will not allow someone to take something that is yours. It will come back to you. As we see with the woman, the child that she birthed, nursed, and cared for, was returned unto her.

Your vision should live at all costs. Your purpose, your destiny, is contingent upon the life of your vision. As long as God is in the forefront, your vision will remain before you and it will live! God is your King, and He will make sure that your vision is in your possession at all times!

Self-Awareness Check

Are you sleeping on your vision?
_____
_____

Have you been operating in things that are not yours?
_____
_____

Identify things in your life that continually fail. Are they truly yours?
_____
_____

What are you willing to give up to ensure your vision lives?
_____
_____

Chapter Seven
Invest In Your Vision

The vision that God gives you is something that is precious not only to you, but to Him. When God gives you something, when He shares something with you, it isn't for you to put it up and keep it for yourself. He purposes His thoughts and gifts to be extraordinary seeds in your life. Whatever He plants into you, He expects a harvest from it. Likewise, you should also expect bountiful blessings not only from the fruit, but even from the root.

Expect A Return

It takes a special kind of person to believe God completely. We hear so many times that if you give, God will give unto you. This sounds good, and it requires a measure of faith. However, this can be risky business to someone who is not used to giving things away.

The society we live in seems to be tossed between two extremes. We are told to save for a rainy day and don't give away the farm. However, we are also told that if you invest in the stock market, there is a chance that you can be rich. It is not guaranteed that you will be rich, and things come up all of the time, so saving doesn't seem to be an option. You may wonder, 'what does this have to do with vision?' Well, it has *much* to do with it!

The vision that God has given you is the key to unlocking prosperity in your life. If you don't put your vision to work for you, then you will never know the potential of the gifts that God has instilled within you. You become a safe investor in yourself. It is safe to just take all that you are given and keep it in a little corner just for yourself. You don't have to endure ridicule from the world, people criticizing your work, giving up on you, and not believing in what God gave you. You think that you know what you possess, but you are content with not sharing it with anyone else.

I would like to submit to you, that if you belong to this segment of Christians who would rather be safe than come into your full potential, that you really do not know what you possess. What you have is so powerful, that the devil will do anything to stop you from accomplishing your purpose. This includes getting you to do something other than your purpose. If you are accomplishing things outside of the will of God, then you are doing nothing to further your purpose. In fact, you are doing exactly what the devil wants you to do. As long as you are not operating in the power that God has given you, no matter how much good you believe you are doing, the devil is happy!

If you realize that because God gave it to you, you can expect nothing less than greatness, then you will be able to operate fully in what God has for you. This means that you will begin to invest your time, energy, and life into what God has given you. If the Lord gave you a dream of counseling people, you will begin by obtaining an education in the area of counseling. You invest your money into making sure that you understand the ins and outs of that profession, all the while using it for the up building of the kingdom of God.

If you invest in something, you expect something in return. God has invested His gifts and talents in you. He expects a return on His investment. In believing God, you should believe that because He expects a return that a return *will* come!

I'm reminded of Matthew chapter 25 where Jesus tells us of the parable of the man giving talents to his servants. He gave them talents according to their *ability*! What God has given you is an indication of what He knows that you can deliver. It's not that He gives you more or less than what He gives someone else; it is what you do with what you have!

As long as you believe and expect a return on what God has given you, you will operate in the realm of supernatural expectation. As long as you can see it, you can literally pull it out of the spiritual realm and allow it to manifest physically.

I know that seems like a lot, but you have to realize the potential and the power that is invested in you. The enemy wants to keep you bound so that you will not realize what God has for you. As you keep your focus on the vision then the path that you should take will become clear.

Your Vision Makes Way for You

The vision that God gives you is like your flashlight through life. It will make roads that are narrow easier to navigate. Proverbs 29:18 tells us:

'Where there is no vision, the people perish'

Plainly put, if there is no direction, no purpose, no vision in your life, what you set out to do will never be accomplished. We all have to have a game plan before anything is executed.

God gave you a vision and He has established a game plan within the vision. As you focus on where you want and need to be, the plan that God has for you will become evident. The plans that He has imparted to you are in place to benefit you.

As you look over the game plan, God will begin to bring back to your remembrance the very thing that He has purposed in your heart for you to do. Once you begin to invest in your vision, you will begin to see your life unfold the way that God created it to.

Once you begin to walk in your vision, others will be inclined to give unto you simply because Gods honors your obedience to the call on your life. Your vision is not only the foundation for your life, but it is a creative vehicle that will attract investors to fuel it to become reality.

Remember back to Habakkuk 2:2 when it says to make the vision plain so that he may run that reads it. Your vision will not only cause a spark in you, but it will cause a spark in others. How will people know to run because of your vision if they are unable to see it?

Understand that there will be people against anything that you do. But do not resign yourself to the idea that *everyone* is against you. God has assigned certain people to cross your path to ensure that your vision becomes a reality. They are there to help you on your way. They will believe in your vision because they believe that God gave it to you.

God doesn't give vision without provision! His provision is so great, and so on time; that you will know without a doubt that it is from God and you will know that He will protect both you and your vision! The thing about God is that He wants to make sure that you realize that whatever He gives you is from Him. What He gives you and when He gives it to you may not make much sense to you or to anyone else. But take comfort in knowing that God knows what He is doing!

Your Path is Not Typical

It is very easy to listen to what someone else has done or seen someone else's accomplishments and then try to model your life after theirs. There are books about the sure fire way to get rich, how to get out of debt, and how to make your money work for you. However, if you are like me, sometimes those things do not work. Why? Because God wants you to know that it is not by your power or might that you have what you have!

You may not have been born into a wealthy family, but that does not mean that you will not accrue wealth. You may not have basketball skills, but that does not mean that you cannot own a team. You may not have a degree, but that does not mean that you can't be an executive. God is known for using common people to do uncommon things!

You could win the lottery and be able to pay your bills, but who would truly get the glory? And how long will the lottery money last? God wants you to take a risk on *Him*! He is the only investment with a guaranteed multiple return. Sometimes this involves taking the road that no one else would dare take. It involves going places and meeting people that everyone else would not go or meet. You have to step out of your comfort zone, and step into the peculiarity that you are as a child of God. 1 Peter 2:9 tells us that we are a peculiar people. That means that what works for others may not work for you. Furthermore, what God allows you to excel in, may not be the avenue that someone else excels in.

There is so much set up for God's children, but too few are willing to go down the unknown path to obtain it. This is where trusting God comes into play. Your road may not be typical. People may not understand how you were battling with some things yesterday, but are on track for what

God has for you today. It is not for everyone else to understand. As long as you know that God gave you the vision, it only matters that you see that the vision becomes a reality.

It will not be easy, but it is also not impossible. Your vision will make way for you on a path that is not typical. Once you are on the path, it is up to you to go onward and upward.

You Will Make Your Way Prosperous

When you focus on the vision for your life, you are actually keeping your mind stayed on God! That takes a seemingly difficult task and puts it in a simple light. If your focus is on your vision, it is actually on God's vision. It will cause you to think on the word of God, meditate, and live your life as God would have you to live. Joshua 1:8 tells us:

'This book of the law shall not depart out of thy mouth; but thou shalt meditate therein day and night, that thou mayest observe to do according to all that is written

therein: for then thou shalt make thy way prosperous, and then thou shalt have good success.'

You may want to read that a couple of more times! Did you grasp that? If you keep your mind stayed on Jesus, if you meditate on His word, if you keep your vision in the forefront, God will allow *you* to make *your* way prosperous!

God lays out the vision, and then you fill in the construction. The vision has to prosper because it is God's investment. He will allow you to go where you want to and do what you want to do. God is not going to keep you bound in a box; He is so much bigger than that. And because He is bigger than that, so are you!

When your thoughts are connected to your purpose, only then will you begin to see prosperity flourish in your life. Think on your vision and you will begin to see the glory of God fill your every thought and be manifested in your actions. It takes action on your part in order for your vision to allow you to make your way prosperous.

But that is not all. The verse goes on to say that you will have good success! It is a process that must be completed before you will find good success in your life. God has to be first. When He is first, you begin to think on the things of God. Then you will make your way prosperous. And finally, you will have good success! I don't know about you, but I have found hope in that verse!

What you are going through, the thoughts that you are bringing under subjection, it is not just to do what God tells you to do. It is to *be* what God has called you to be! God pours His spirit out to you so that you have all that you need in order to live the life of His child! These are the keys to successfully living your vision as well as successfully *living*!

Once again, it takes a special person to believe in God. God has anointed you to be that special person because He has entrusted you with a vision that He knows will yield a great return. That return not only benefits Him, but it benefits you as an heir. Investing in your vision and in yourself is an act of investing in your very own inheritance.

You can now successfully live your vision. Know that you came and will still go a mighty long way. Remember, it's not impossible to get there, because through Jesus Christ, *all* things are possible!

Self-Awareness Check

Do you expect a return when you work your vision?
_____
_____
_____

Who has God placed in your life to further your vision?
_____
_____
_____

Identify unique skills that God has equipped you with.
_____
_____
_____

Can you see how your vision will prosper you? How?
_____
_____
_____

Chapter Eight
From Bondage to Freedom

It is a humbling experience when you have stepped out of the chains of bondage and into freedom. Looking over all that you have been through, it is more than a testament to the strength that God has given you; it is a testament to who you are in Christ. No longer being defined by what you have been through is liberty within itself. Allowing God to take you from chains to release will help to you to breathe easier. But it does not stop there.

Defined By Your Purpose

Your identity is at stake with every decision that you make and every step that you take. What you do is how people identify you. It isn't enough to just know what God has made you to be. You have to take what you know and put your thoughts into action. Don't just think that you are free, begin living because you are free!

When you are set free, you are free indeed! Indeed means that you are not free from just a specific area of your life, but that you are free from everything. God is not going to free you from debt and then neglect other areas of your finances. When He frees you, the slate is wiped clean. God doesn't see you as someone who has gotten into so much trouble that He has to keep saving you from them. He is your Savior, and He has your back at all times. That is not the issue. The issue is your purpose!

When God looks at you, He sees purpose. He sees who you truly are and where you are going. What He wants you to do is see yourself the way that He sees you. When you are free mentally of things that can hinder you, you become free to be you!

Your purpose is the foundation of who you are. If you were purposed to be a doctor, then people should look at you be able to identify you as a doctor. How? They see the work that you do, your appearance, and the way that you talk. These should all reflect your purpose. It should reflect who you are: a doctor!

I'm reminded of Peter when he denied Jesus three times. He tried his best to not be identified with Jesus, but his very speech *betrayed* him! He walked in his purpose so successfully, that he couldn't even pretend to be someone other than who he was. This is how we should be defined. Even if you try to do something other than what you are purposed to do, someone should be able to look at you and still see your purpose.

Align Your Life With Your Purpose

Walking in your purpose requires your thoughts, heart, and actions to be aligned together. Everything working together in harmony will allow you to be who you are in Christ. When you think a thing, you can dismiss it or create it with action. We must know when to dismiss a thought and when to create the thought!

Taking your thoughts under subjection takes focus and practice. There are suggestions and messages that enter your mind daily. Most of them are unhealthy and will cause you to dwell on things that are outside of your purpose. Dwelling on them will often times lead to actions that are harmful and contradictory to who you are.

God has given us the ability to discern what is harmful and what is helpful. You know what is right and what is wrong. We get into trouble because it is so much easier to dismiss the right and create the wrong. This is a great starting point, because it takes knowledge in order to change something.

As you operate in a free mindset, you will be able to dismiss the thoughts before you are tempted to put them into action. Pay attention to what you think! You will be surprised at what goes into your mind and the temptations used to bring about unhealthy thoughts.

Creation of good thoughts is where we need to be. When the functions of the whole body work together for a common cause, it is the perfect filtration system. As you dismiss the harmful thoughts, you can focus on the thoughts that God would have you dwell on. When you focus on thoughts in relation to your purpose, unhealthy thoughts will not have a chance to enter into your mind.

Dwelling on good things, dwelling on God will keep you in perfect peace. This peace will allow you to forget the things that are behind and press toward the mark that God has called you to. You will then begin to create what God has spoken into you. You will walk in your purpose and you will be defined by your walk.

The Chains Are Broken

Being defined by your walk will bring about happiness to your life. However, sometimes we come to a place where we are working what God has given us, but slip back to where we used to be.

All of us have been there. We get ourselves out of something and for some reason find ourselves back in the same bind. We have to realize that when God frees us, the chains are broken! You don't have to go back and God has given you the provision to keep you from going back.

There is always a tug from that past that seems to be ever present in our lives. That trip down memory lane is helpful as it reminds you of where you have been. But, sometimes, that trip can land people outside of the will of God. Handcuffs can leave a mark on the wrists if they are on too tight. This is what mental bondage can do to us. We can see the imprint of what was and it is a constant reminder of who we used to be. Even when the handcuffs are removed, you may sometimes still feel the effect of the bondage. The memory is there to keep you from wanting to be bound again.

We wonder why when someone has been living free from alcohol for 5 years, they go to a party and have just one drink, and suddenly they can't let go anymore. It isn't the one drink that sends them out of control; it is the effect that the drink once had on them that takes their mind off of their accomplishment and back onto the addiction. Nothing can keep you bound if you don't allow it to. Once your mind is continually on your purpose you will create what God has instilled inside of you. The past will be a memory, but it won't matter anymore. Your past is where you came from; your vision is where you are going to.

The chains are broken, you are free, but you have to know within your heart that you are free. What used to bind you can no longer have a hold on you because God freed you indeed. The cost has been paid; Jesus died on the cross so that you can experience freedom in every area of your life. The liberty that He has given you from that act of love carries a key with it. No matter what comes your way, that key cannot be taken from you. You always will have the provision to unlock freedom at any time. The power of God is strong enough to loose any chain and its sustaining power will keep them loosed!

Don't Give Place to the Enemy

When you become free in the Lord, do not be fooled into thinking that the enemy will leave you alone. When your mind is stayed on Jesus, the devil's devices will be of no effect on you, but he is still able to affect the things that are *around* you!

It is so important that you recognize that things will come against you. People will not like what you are doing and old friends won't stick with you. However, what you do for God is the only thing that will last. If you accomplish something outside of the will of God for your life, you really did not accomplish anything. But as you focus on your vision, you will further your purpose with every action that you create. It takes your purpose to propel you to your destiny; it is something that you have to protect because trouble is on every side. Although trouble is on every side, it does not have to stop you.

If you hear things that have a purpose to distract or destroy you, you have to weigh it against your purpose. You must discern if it is worth your time and energy to even think about. The tools of the devil are anger, gossip, backbiting, etc. If these things seem to be creeping up around you, it is your responsibility to shut them down.

All the enemy needs is an avenue to get you to be distracted from your vision and he will take it so that he can remove power from you. The devil's purpose is to steal, kill, and destroy, but the Holy Spirit replenishes, renews, and rebuilds so that you can continue to walk in what God gives you.

Going from slavery to freedom is not the easiest transition. As a slave, you are restricted in what you do. You have a huge amount of potential but no arena to exercise it. As a people, we are used to being restrained and not allowed to fulfill our dreams. Or, it takes a large amount of hoops to jump through in order to take one step in getting to be who we want to be.

Freedom gives you liberty to not only think of great things, but make great things happen. God has given you that freedom. Take it for what it is, do the will of God, and you will see prosperity reign in your life. Don't allow the enemy to come in and destroy what you have worked so hard for. You are free, now you have to stay free!

Self-Awareness Check

Can you clearly identify your purpose?
_____
_____
_____

Think on 3 issues going on in your life. Are those thoughts healthy?
_____
_____
_____

What memories keep you from wanting to do things that you used to do?
_____
_____
_____

Are you beginning to feel free? What has changed?
_____
_____
_____

Chapter Nine
Keeping Your Freedom

It feels good to fully realize and operate in the freedom that God has given you. Knowing that you are doing what you are called to do provides a sense of fulfillment like no other. Things begin to fall into place and the outcome is just how you expect and imagine it to be. In a perfect world, you would be able to live your vision and not worry about anything.

Fear

God instructs us in Philippians 4:6 to not worry about anything but to trust completely in Him. This should be something that we are able to do without thinking about it. However, there is a thing called fear that creeps up every now and then that desires to distract you from your destiny.

Fear is the lack of trust in God. It is a spirit that is designed to keep you from doing the will of God, therefore keeping you in darkness. Fear can grasp someone operating fully in their vision and persuade them to do something else. This is why you find some people doing so well in an area one day, but seem to be completely miserable the next. Fear takes over and creates an irrational thought that maybe this is not for me.

Fear is a state that can make the strongest person become a weakling. It can turn your brightest day into a gloomy night. It can make you turn your back on the very thing that is there to help you; your *vision*!

Discovering your purpose and walking in it not only takes time, but it takes persistence, dedication, and a spirit of striving for excellence. Because it takes time, fear can come in and cause you to think that you will never accomplish your full vision. It's good to know that it is God's time and not your own, but when you are living free, God's time has to become your time.

That sounds easier said than done, but that is because a lot of people say it instead of simply *doing* it! Fear can be alleviated in your life! God has given you three tools to kill fear and continue to feed life into your vision. 1 Timothy 1:7 tells us:

For God hath not given us the spirit of fear; but of power, and of love, and of a sound mind.

Power

God has instilled in you a vision that will turn this world upside down. It will help to build the kingdom of God and His people. God would not equip you with vision and not supply you with power. He has given you the ability to accomplish the very thing that He has planted in your heart.

What you have envisioned in your heart, you will be able to make a reality. This is not something that you *may* be able to do. But it is something that you *can* and *will* do. This power is inclusive of strength, persistence, and determination.

We can spend so many hours working for someone and doing things that contribute nothing to our purpose. Imagine what you could do when you operate in the power that you are given and use it for its specific purpose!

There is confidence that comes from doing something that you know that you were created to do. No one can do it like you and even if they tried, they could not produce the same results. This is the power that is available to you.

Fear has a hard time battling power. Someone who is confident in their ability is not afraid to take on a task in which they know that they can successfully complete. God has given you power, and that power covers anything that would try to come against you. There is little space for timidity in a confident person. Their walk, talk, and action breeds power!

Jesus was able to go anywhere that He desired and talk to even those who sought to kill Him because He knew who He was! He had confidence that He had a purpose that had to be fulfilled and He was the only one to fulfill it. Power was present wherever He walked. He didn't have time to be afraid, because He had a work to do.

You should walk in that same confidence. You are free indeed. That means you don't have to be in bondage. Power has been released in the form of your vision and it blocks the spirit of fear from manifesting itself in your life. You have to believe that you are somebody. Believe that you have been given power and the spirit of power will go into battle against the spirit of fear. Know that power is the victor every time!

Love

God loves you so much and He wants you to depend on nothing but Him. He wants you to benefit from what He gives you and He wants you to recognize that it comes from Him. Succumbing to God's love and allowing God to love you will put you in the realm of unending freedom.

Where there is love, there is no fear of harm. This, of course, comes in the form of relationship. God desires a two-way relationship with you. It is one thing for God to love you and keep you from harm; it is another thing to be completely reciprocal in that love and forming a strong relationship.

Oftentimes we can get caught up in what is going on around us and then neglect the relationship that we have with God. If you don't nurture that relationship, you can forget that you are free and that is another avenue where fear can plant itself in your life.

You would think that it is hard to forget to love God. He has given you so much; He has brought you through so many storms, so how can you forget Him? Well, it happens daily! Without going into how you forget about Him during the course of the day, you should be able to pinpoint how you miss the opportunities to love on God. Keeping your mind stayed on Jesus will keep you in perfect peace.

There is peace that comes just when you say the name Jesus because your spirit recognizes the lover of your soul! When you truly love someone, there is no fear of them leaving or of you being alone. Love provides divine protection for the heart and mind. Without love, you are vulnerable to every spirit that is harmful to you especially fear.

Fear feeds off of those who feel alone. It creates a need to hold onto anything or anyone just so the loneliness will go away. This is a dangerous situation and the reason why so many people try to find love or protection in people that are not equipped to provide them with love! Not just anyone can handle your heart! Not just anyone can provide complete protection for you! Only Jesus is designed and purposed to be that for you. He then created others to love you as your vision comes to reality.

When love is around you, you feel safe. The spirit of love will go to battle against the spirit of fear. Know that love is the victor every time!

Sound Mind

God also gives you a sound mind. When you are sound in mind, you are level headed and you possess a great amount of discipline. Freedom allows you to think clearly. You are not clouded with what is going on around you, but you have a clear focus of the task at hand.

Judgment and decision- making is so important when you are operating in freedom. The choices that you make can bring life to your vision or can be detrimental to your life. God has given you the ability to make wise choices.

There are things in your life that are purposed to throw you off track and to make you do things that you used to do. But when you have a sound mind, you will not rush into things. Even if things are thrown at you, you are able to manage not only those things, but your response to those things.

Your response to a matter is the foundation of what happens next. If you are irrational in how you respond to something, then the outcome will be chaotic. However, if you are calm and clear headed, you will be able to better handle any situation that comes your way.

Fear wants to catch you in an irrational state so that it can bring about chaos to your newly found freedom. When you have freedom, you shouldn't feel overburdened with life. However, freedom allows you to wisely manage your life as well as your vision.

A person who carries a lot of burdens can become ineffective. They have too many things that they have to accomplish at once, they move slowly, and their decisions are often for the short-term instead of the long-term. Your mind has to be clear in order to remain free. A clear mind can distinguish what is needed and what is just extra weight.

A person who is disciplined is one who possesses a sound mind. As you operate in freedom, there must be order in your life. I'm not saying that you have to be a predictable and boring person. But I am saying that you have to know what you are doing.
Goals must be set for yourself and then there must be action present in accomplishing those goals.

As you outline your vision, you should be able to know where you are and where you are going. Fear is present when there is uncertainty. As long as you know where you are going, what comes your way should not take you off track. Your focus should be on the goal and doing what it takes to get there.

God has given you the spirit of a sound mind. As you operate in freedom, the spirit of a sound mind will go to battle against the spirit of fear. Know that a sound mind is the victor every time!

You Are Free

Knowing that you are free is a gift that God has given you. He desires that you are free and not bound to anything that is meant to harm you. You now recognize your purpose and are working towards your God-given vision. That is a freedom that a lot of people will never get to experience.

When you know who you are in God, you will realize that you don't have to live how others expect you to live. God breaks down any wall, barrier, stereotype, or low expectations that anyone would dare put up before you. As a child of God, you should know nothing but freedom!

Take comfort in knowing that when God sets you free, you are free indeed! The chains have been loosed and have fallen to the floor. The next thing that you have to do is to get up and walk away from the chains. You have to begin walking towards your vision and God will light your path.

It may seem dark at first, but as you begin living your purpose, the vision will become clearer and clearer. The vision that was cloudy at first will soon be in focus. What was black and white will now be vivid color. God is taking you to new levels. Your mind is now free to do the work that you are called to do. This cycle has been broken. Your name is not bondage, your name is freedom!

Self-Awareness Check

What is your vision?

_____

_____

_____

What had you bound in the past?

_____

_____

_____

Do you believe that God has set you free?

_____

_____

_____

Where do you want to go from here?

_____

_____

_____

About The Author

Pastor Nikesha Luther originates from St. Louis, MO. She received a Bachelor's degree in Social Work from Columbia College. She is currently an Auto Underwriter for State Farm Insurance.

Pastor Luther was ordained under her husband, Bishop Darrell Luther. She preaches with the anointing of prophecy and the determination to reach those who do not know Jesus Christ as their Lord and Savior. Pastor Luther strives to be a vessel that will implement change and cause an atmospheric revelation to those who hear.

Pastor Luther is the founder of 'Worth A Change', a ministry that seeks to delve into the life of the modern woman of God. This ministry unlocks emotions which lead to uninhibited sharing among women who would not normally do so. This ministry will bring women closer together while helping them to understand their individual purpose and walk into their destiny!

Bishop and Pastor Luther are the proud parents of three sons, Darrell Dwayne Jr., Daniel Bradley, and Micah Dwayne.

Other books by CECO Publishing:

In *From Promise to Delivery* Elder LaToya Stevens discusses how as believers, we often wonder why we don't see the promises God has made us come to pass. This book will help the reader identify what is stopping them from conceiving, carrying, and delivering the promises of God.

To purchase go to: www.cecofellowship.org/Store.html

www.ingramcontent.com/pod-product-compliance
Lightning Source LLC
Chambersburg PA
CBHW021014090426
42738CB00007B/780